VAN TIL:
THE
THEOLOGIAN

JOHN   FRAME

D1292915

PILGRIM PUBLISHING COMPANY
CHATTANOOGA, TENNESSEE

International Standard Book Number: 0-916034-02-X
Library of Congress Catalog Card Number: 75-36460
Manufactured in the United States of America

In 1961, Cornelius Van Til reviewed a book by R. H. Bremmer called *Herman Bavinck als Dogmaticus* (*Herman Bavinck the Theologian*).[1] Having run across this review in a recent perusal of the Van Til corpus, I asked myself whether someday there might be a book called *Cornelius Van Til als Dogmaticus*.

Perhaps one's first instinct would be to say no. Van Til, after all, is an apologist, not a dogmatician. He did indeed teach courses in systematic theology for many years, but those courses (if some of his former students are to be believed) were essentially apologetics courses in disguise. Where Van Til does discuss theological issues, furthermore, he includes little exegesis (in the traditional sense of that term). What exegesis he does present is usually borrowed from other sources. His dogmatic formulations, too, are often simple repetitions or paraphrases of the creeds and of the great Reformed theologians from Calvin onward. Even when Van Til's theology sounds most strange to American ears (for example, his strong emphasis upon the ethical/metaphysical distinction), he is very often paraphrasing ideas from the Dutch tradition. (In the case of the ethical/metaphysical distinction, the source is Bavinck.)

If, however, from the above considerations we conclude that Van Til's theology is uninteresting and/or unimportant, we will merely expose ourselves as shallow thinkers and cut ourselves off from one whose contribution to theology is of virtually Copernican dimensions. If Van Til had done nothing more than to introduce some of the best insights of the Dutch theologians to the American public, even then his work would have been of substantial importance. But when one considers the uniqueness of his apologetic position and then further considers the implications of that apologetic for theology, one searches for superlatives to describe the significance of Van Til's overall approach.

Van Til's apologetics may well be described as a group of original applications of some familiar Reformed doctrines. In Van Til's view, apologetics and theology (particularly systematic theology) are very closely

---

1. C. Van Til, "Bavinck the Theologian, A Review Article," *Westminster Theological Journal* XXIV, 1 (November, 1961), 1-17. Incidentally, this article is important in that, so far as I can tell, it is Van Til's first serious written criticism of Herman Dooyeweerd.

related: ". . . defense and positive statement go hand in hand."[2] There can be no adequate positive statement without defense against error, and *vice versa*. In fact, "Systematic Theology is more closely related to apologetics than are any of the other disciplines. In it we have the system of truth that we are to defend."[3] Thus Van Til begins the exposition of his apologetic with an outline of Reformed systematic theology.[4] It is clear from the outset that one of Van Til's basic concerns is to present an apologetic which is true to Scripture and Reformed doctrine. His major complaints against competing apologetic methods are theological complaints, that is, that they compromise the incomprehensibility of God, total depravity, the clarity of natural revelation, God's comprehensive control over creation, and so on. His appeal to the non-Christian contains much exposition of Reformed doctrine, in order that the unbeliever might know *what sort of* God is being argued for.[5] Thus, Gordon R. Lewis[6] and John W. Montgomery[7] charge that Van Til *confuses* apologetics with systematic theology. This criticism is mistaken, for it suggests that Van Til would merely proclaim doctrine to a non-Christian without evidence or argument. Even though "defense and positive statement go hand in hand," Van Til is quite capable of distinguishing between them, and he is self-consciously concerned to supplement the one with the other.[8] Yet the Lewis-Montgomery criticism shows a real insight into the structure of Van Til's thought, for in one sense it is indeed difficult to distinguish apologetics from systematic theology in Van Til's position. Though Van Til does clearly distinguish "positive statement" from "defense," and though in general he aligns the first with theology and the second with apologetics, he does insist that, because each is indispensable to the other, theology must have an apologetic thrust, and apologetics must expound theology. The difference between the two in practice, then, becomes a *difference in emphasis* rather than of subject matter.

This practical identification of the two disciplines makes Van Til's apologetics highly responsive to the demands of Reformed doctrine. But

---

2. Van Til, *Apologetics* (Syllabus, 1959), 3.

3. *Ibid.*, 4.

4. *Ibid.*, 4ff; cf. Van Til, *The Defense of the Faith* (Philadelphia: Presbyterian and Reformed, 1955), 23ff.

5. Note, for example, the treatment of creation, providence, prophecy, and miracle in Van Til's pamphlet, *Why I Believe in God* (Philadelphia: Orthodox Presbyterian Church, n.d.), 13-15.

6. In E. Geehan, ed., *Jerusalem and Athens* (Nutley, N. J.: Presbyterian and Reformed, 1971), 349.

7. In *ibid.*, 391f.

8. Van Til, *Apologetics*, 3f.; *Why I Believe in God*, 16. The idea that Van Til's apologetic substitutes proclamation for argument is frequently denied in Van Til's writings, but is nevertheless one of the most prevalent misunderstandings of his position.

the converse is also true: the traditional doctrines take on, in many cases, a very new appearance when put to Van Til's apologetic use. Unoriginal as his doctrinal formulations may be, his *use* of those formulations—his *application* of them—is often quite remarkable. The sovereignty of God becomes an epistemological, as well as a religious and metaphysical principle. The Trinity becomes the answer to the philosophical problem of the one and the many. Common grace becomes the key to a Christian philosophy of history.[9] These new applications of familiar doctrines inevitably increase our understanding of the doctrines themselves, for we come thereby to a new appreciation of what these doctrines demand of us. Sometimes these new understandings are of quite a radical sort—radical enough to require new formulations, or at least supplementary formulations, of the doctrines themselves. Van Til, as we have observed, rarely provides such revised formulations, though he does at some significant points, as we shall see. But there is much in Van Til that will require future orthodox Reformed dogmaticians to rethink much of the traditional language and thus to go beyond Van Til himself. Not that the traditional language is wrong (generally speaking); it is just that through reading Van Til we often become painfully aware of how much more needs to be said.

Thus, Van Til's theology, conventional and traditional as it may seem at first glance, is just as significant in its own way as is his apologetics. If Van Til has given a new epistemological self-consciousness to apologetics, then he has done the same for theology and all other types of Christian thought. If (as may well be said) Van Til has done for Christian thought what Kant accomplished for non-Christian thought, giving it a revolutionary awareness of the uniqueness and comprehensiveness of its distinctive principles, then as with Kant the "Copernican" radicalism of his contribution must be appreciated in all areas of human thought and life.

This paper attempts to set forth the contributions of Van Til to theology, both the "explicit" and the "implicit" ones. As suggested above, the importance of Van Til's contribution does not always lie on the surface. At times the logic of his position requires us to go beyond his explicit teachings, to say more than he himself says. I intend to suggest some areas where such is the case and also to suggest clarifications and corrections in Van Til's formulations where the genius of his own thought demands them.[10]

---

9. For references and further discussion on these matters, see below.

10. Here let me say a word on behalf of the need for *constructive critical analysis* of Van Til. Van Til, like any human thinker, is fallible. Those who love and honor him can pay him no higher service than to help him see his own weaknesses and thereby to increase the effectiveness of his future efforts. We must therefore be

Where shall we begin? In this sort of paper, one is often torn between focusing upon a thinker's *basic concerns* and focusing on his *distinctive teachings*. The two are not always the same. Van Til's concern is to be faithful to the biblical gospel: the sovereignty of God, the authority of Scripture, the reality of Christ's redemptive work in history, etc. But these concerns are also the concerns of many others—Augustine, Calvin, Kuyper, Warfield, many more. If we portray Van Til as, say, a "theologian of divine sovereignty," then how do we distinguish him from Calvin? Is it that Van Til is *more* concerned for divine sovereignty than was Calvin? Doubtful. Is it that Van Til *does more justice* to divine sovereignty than does Calvin? Well, perhaps. But if so, how does he do it? What we want to know is not so much what Van Til's concerns are, for these are obvious to anyone who reads Van Til, and are in any case the common property of the whole Christian church. We want to know, rather, how Van Til is able uniquely to implement these concerns in certain areas of controversy. What is it that is *distinctive* to Van Til? What does he do that Calvin, say, does not? Therefore, this paper will focus, not on Van Til's "basic concerns," but on his "distinctive teachings." The reader should be warned, however, that such a focus may distort the

---

greatly saddened by the fact that there has been *almost no* quality critical work done on Van Til's writings from sources sympathetic to his position. (a) Most critical work on Van Til has come from sources deeply *un*sympathetic to him—from "debunkers." Note in this connection James Daane, *A Theology of Grace* (Grand Rapids: Eerdmans, 1954), the contributions of Montgomery and Pinnock in *Jerusalem and Athens,* and many more. (b) Most *sympathetic* responses to Van Til have been utterly uncritical and generally non-analytical. They simply laud Van Til's positions and castigate his opponents without any serious wrestling with the issues Van Til raises. Such writers mean to do him tribute, yet meek acquiescence is hardly an adequate response, certainly no compliment, to a thinker who means to challenge us at the most profound intellectual and spiritual level. As an example of this tendency, note D. Vickers' review of *Jerusalem and Athens,* in *Westminster Theological Journal* XXXIV, 2 (May, 1972), 174-179. (c) A third group, the cosmonomic idea thinkers, has taken a middle ground, mingling appreciation of Van Til with criticism. Yet their critique of Van Til rests on a rather bizarre misinterpretation of his teaching—a misinterpretation resulting from their attempt to squeeze Van Til's thought into the rigid categories of their philosophical scheme. Cf. the contributions of Dooyeweerd and Knudsen in *Jerusalem and Athens.* (d) The best material on Van Til comes from the Chalcedon group—R. J. Rushdoony, Gary North, Gregory Bahnsen, and a few others such as Vern Poythress, a recent graduate of Westminster Seminary. These alone have made a truly creative use of Van Til's work, building on what he has done, applying it to areas which Van Til himself has not considered. We expect much of this in the present volume. Such *applications* of Van Til are most useful in themselves and provide implicitly an analytical perspective, thus distinguishing themselves from those treatments noted under (b). But this last group, like group (b), has generally refrained from criticism. Perhaps these men feel that they are better equipped to "apply" than to "critically analyze." But *someone* ought to get busy on the latter job. *Semper reformanda!* Great as Van Til's achievement is, the mind boggles at how much greater it might have been if Van Til had been surrounded by loving, appreciative, yet critically perceptive, fellow apologists.

shape of Van Til's system in a certain way. It may seem from this treatment that Van Til's thought is preoccupied with abstractions—unity and diversity, paradox and logic, analogy, epistemology, etc. Such, however, would be a false impression. These "abstract" concerns are fairly high on the list of Van Tillian "distinctives," but fairly low on a list of his "basic concerns." Van Til pursues such philosophical questions only in order to be faithful in his witness to Jesus Christ. *Far from being "preoccupied" with such abstractions, Van Til brings them up with reluctance, and only as a means of showing the implications of the gospel of God's saving grace.*

As I have hinted in the above caveat, I find Van Til's major distinctiveness in the area of theological introduction or "meta-theology"—the theology of theology, the study of theological method and structure. This area is sometimes called "theological prolegomena," a term which designates those things which must be "said before" theology may be done. Sometimes "prolegomena" is conceived of as not properly belonging to a theological system. Louis Berkhof and others fail to include the doctrine of Scripture in their major dogmatic works, relegating that doctrine to supplementary or "introductory" volumes, since they feel, apparently, that the doctrine of Scripture belongs to "prolegomena" and not to theology. Whatever may be said on behalf of this procedure, a "Van Tillian theologian" will wish to guard strongly against any implication that "prolegomena" is some kind of autonomous rational activity which *precedes* the believer's submission of his mind to God's Word. "Prolegomena" must be just as subject to Scripture as any area of theology—especially so, since prolegomena so greatly influences *every* phase of theological thinking. *All* our thoughts, "introductory" and otherwise, must be captive to the obedience of Christ (II Cor. 10:5). Thus I insist that in *one* sense, perhaps the most important sense, "prolegomena" is a properly theological discipline.

Yet prolegomena, or theological introduction,[11] deals with many matters which are more often associated with philosophy than with theology: questions of epistemology, of logic, of analogy, and so on. Distinctive to Van Til's thought in this area is a generalized reflection upon the *relation of unity to diversity* in the theological organism. In my view, Van Til is the first orthodox Christian thinker to have studied this question in a distinctively theological way. This is what I take to be *Van Til's most distinctive contribution to theology.* Only a man with his philosophical background could have attacked such a problem, but only a man with

---

11. I prefer the second designation for reasons discussed in the previous paragraph. So does Van Til, although, so far as I know, he has never explicitly stated the argument I have presented.

his profoundly biblical commitment could have adopted his distinctive approach.

In the rest of this paper, I shall discuss Van Til's concept of the Christian "system of truth." The analysis will focus on the various sorts of "unities" and "diversities" to be found among the various Christian doctrines. In particular, I shall ask in what ways the various doctrines are "interdependent"—in what ways they "require one another"—and, on the other hand, in what sense these doctrines are "paradoxically" related. In the course of the discussion, I concern myself not merely with these methodological questions. I will explore many of Van Til's specific doctrinal teachings, some in passing, others at length.

Is there a "system" of Christian truth? Surely that is an important "introductory" consideration to theology, especially systematic theology! It has been a controversial question: Kierkegaard and Barth have condemned the very idea of a doctrinal "system" as an affront to God, as a human attempt to master and manipulate God's revelation. On the other hand, E. J. Carnell set forth something called "systematic consistency" as the final test of religious truth.[12] What does Van Til say? Typically, his answer carries with it a demand for further analysis: it all depends on what you mean by "system." In one sense, yes, there is such a system; in another sense, no. Thus, at times Van Til appears unequivocally to endorse the idea of "system," while at other times he seems to attack it.

I. Pro-System

Van Til's endorsement of "system" begins with the consideration that God himself is "exhaustively comprehensible to himself."[13] God's self-knowledge is in no way defective; it is in perfect order. And to say this is to say, in one sense, that God's knowledge is "systematic": ". . . there must be in God an absolute system of knowledge."[14] This knowledge includes knowledge not only of God himself but also of His works. Since God has planned and controls all things, "All created reality therefore actually displays this plan. It is, in consequence, inherently rational."[13] *God, therefore, has a "systematic" knowledge of himself and of the world, since He knows His own plan exhaustively and since the world perfectly conforms to that plan.*

---

12. E. J. Carnell, *An Introduction to Christian Apologetics* (Grand Rapids: Eerdmans, 1948), 56ff.

13. Van Til, "Nature and Scripture," in N. Stonehouse and P. Woolley, ed., *The Infallible Word* (Philadelphia: Presbyterian and Reformed, 3rd revised printing, 1967), 277.

14. Van Til, *The Defense of the Faith,* 61. Cf. "God is absolute rationality. He was and is the only self-contained whole, the system of absolute truth," *An Introduction to Systematic Theology* (Syllabus, 1961), 10.

Because of this absolute divine system of truth, *true knowledge is available to men.* God has created the world and us, adapting each to the other according to His rational plan. "We see then that our knowledge of the universe must be true since we are creatures of God who has made both us and the universe."[14] God's rationality vindicates human knowledge: "We say that if there is to be any true knowledge at all there must be in God an absolute system of knowledge."[14] This human knowledge is not "exhaustive" or "comprehensive"; only God has that sort of knowledge. But it is, or is capable of being, genuinely true.[15] Even more: with regard to "the existence of God and the truth of Christian theism," there is "absolutely certain proof."[16] Not only do we have *true* knowledge of God, but *certain* knowledge as well. God is *clearly* revealed, so that His existence and the truth of His word is not just "possible" or "probable," but certain.[17] There *is* a cogent "theistic proof."[18]

This knowledge of God available to man is "systematic" in two related senses. In the first place, it is "systematic" in the sense of being *internally coherent:*

> But I do, of course, confess that what Scripture teaches may properly be spoken of as a system of truth. God identifies the Scriptures as his Word. And he himself, as he tells us, exists as an internally self-coherent being. His revelation of himself to man cannot be anything but internally coherent. When therefore the Bible teaches that God controls by his plan, whatever comes to pass, it does not also teach that God does not control whatever comes to pass. If such were the case, God's promises and threats would be meaningless.[19]

There is no "real contradiction" in God's revelation. It cannot be the case that "the same ultimate will of God wills, and yet wills not, the salvation of sinners."[20] There can be no "contradiction between the secret and revealed wills of God."[21] Note also:

---

15. Van Til, *An Introduction to Systematic Theology,* 24, 164; *The Defense of the Faith,* 60; "Nature and Scripture," 277.

16. Van Til, *The Defense of the Faith,* 120; *Apologetics,* 64.

17. Van Til, *An Introduction to Systematic Theology,* 114f.; *Apologetics,* 13; "Nature and Scripture," 278f.

18. Van Til, *An Introduction to Systematic Theology,* 102ff., 196; *The Defense of the Faith,* 196; *A Christian Theory of Knowledge* (Nutley, N. J.: Presbyterian and Reformed, 1969), 292; *Common Grace and the Gospel* (Nutley, N. J.: Presbyterian and Reformed, 1972), 179ff., 190ff. In this note I have indulged in a bit of referential overkill, because this point is often missed. Van Til is not simply opposed to the theistic proofs as students often imagine. On the contrary, he gives them strong endorsement. But he insists that they be formulated in a distinctively Christian way, rejecting any "proof" based on a non-Christian epistemology.

19. Van Til, *The Defense of the Faith,* 205. Cf. *A Christian Theory of Knowledge,* 38f.

20. Van Til, *Common Grace and the Gospel,* 76.

21. Van Til, *An Introduction to Systematic Theology,* 251.

God can reveal only that which is consistent with his nature as a self-identified being. The law of identity in human logic must be seen to be resting upon the character of God and therefore upon the authoritative revelation of God. But to say that God is both omnipotent and not omnipotent, because conditioned by the ultimate determinations of his creatures, is to remove the very foundation of the law of identity. This is irrationalism. It allows the legitimacy of the non-Christian principle of individuation, namely chance.[22]

Related to this internal coherence of God's revelation is a slightly different sense in which the revelation may be said to be "systematic": there are *relations of dependence* among biblical doctrines. Some may be said to be "fundamental" to others. Some, in fact, are "fundamental" to the whole system.

Naturally, in the system of theology and in apologetics the *doctrine of God* is of fundamental importance. *In apologetics it must always be the final if not the first point of attack.* In theology the main questions deal with the existence and the nature of God.[23]

Fundamental to everything orthodox is the presupposition of the antecedent self-existence of God and of his infallible revelation of himself to man in the Bible.[24]

First and foremost among the attributes, we therefore mention the independence or self-existence of God. . . .[25]

Another "central" doctrine is the historical fall of Adam: only if we take the fall as historical can a sound theology be maintained.[26] "Temporal creation" is another doctrine with which "Christianity stands or falls."[27] Furthermore, predestination, as Warfield says, is the "central doctrine of the Reformation."[28] And the Trinity is the "heart of Christianity."[29]

More specifically, there are doctrines which Van Til sets forth as necessitating other doctrines:

. . . the Christian-theistic conception of an absolute God and an absolute Christ and an absolute Scripture go hand in hand. We cannot accept one without accepting the others.[30]

Self-contained God implies self-attesting revelation.[31] The doctrine of

---

22. Van Til, *A Christian Theory of Knowledge*, 202, cf. 38f.

23. Van Til, *Apologetics*, 4 (emphasis his). Cf. *A Christian Theory of Knowledge*, 12, *The Defense of the Faith*, 59.

24. Van Til, *An Introduction to Systematic Theology*, 1.

25. *Ibid.*, 206.

26. Van Til, *An Introduction to Systematic Theology*, 29.

27. Van Til, *The Defense of the Faith*, 229.

28. Van Til, *The Theology of James Daane* (Philadelphia: Presbyterian and Reformed, 1959), 76.

29. Van Til, *The Defense of the Faith*, 28.

30. Van Til, *Christian-Theistic Ethics* (n.p.: den Dulk Foundation, 1971), 28.

31. Van Til, *The Defense of the Faith*, 203; cf. *An Introduction to Systematic Theology*, 62, "Introduction," to B. B. Warfield, *The Inspiration and Authority of the Bible* (Philadelphia: Presbyterian and Reformed, 1948), 36f., *A Christian Theory of Knowledge*, 70.

analogical knowledge is a "corollary" from the doctrine of the Trinity.[32] Man's knowledge is true "because," not in spite of, the fact that it is "analogical."[32] Man's being and action are genuinely his own "because of" (again, not "in spite of") "the more ultimate being and activity on the part of the will of God."[33] The *personality of God* (and hence the ultimately *personal character of man's environment*) becomes the key to avoiding determinist and indeterminist conceptions[34]—a somewhat surprising idea at first glance, but worked out cogently by Van Til. For one thing, denial of the self-sufficient holiness of God entails denial also of temporal creation and historical Fall.[35] For another, "God is free not in spite of but because of the necessity of his nature."[36] Therefore, "deny the doctrine of creation and you have denied the Christian concept of God."[37] The creation of man in God's image is at the same time a "presupposition of revelation" and a "corollary from the notion of an absolutely self-conscious God."[38]

Van Til's stress on the interdependence of biblical doctrines can be seen from the following examples of his reasoning. The providential involvement of God in all created things and events, His all-foreordaining direction of the world (so characteristic of Reformed theology), requires a distinctively Reformed view of Scripture.[39] To deny biblical authority is to assert one's autonomy or independence of God's control.[40] The differences between Calvinism and Arminianism require a difference in apologetic method.[41] Christian ethics presupposes double predestination.[42] To deny the historicity of the fall is to deny the directness of revelation in history.[43] Modernism, Barthianism,[44] and Arminianism, because of their distinctive teachings, cannot do justice to the biblical

32. Van Til, *A Survey of Christian Epistemology* (n.p.: den Dulk Foundation, 1969), 48; cf. 97.

33. Van Til, *Apologetics*, 11.

34. Van Til, *A Survey of Christian Epistemology*, 67f.; *Christian-Theistic Ethics*, 35, 48. Note also the account of the centrality of God's absolute personality in *The Defense of the Faith*, 29, 59.

35. Van Til, *An Introduction to Systematic Theology*, 244.

36. *Ibid.*, 177.

37. Van Til, *The Defense of the Faith*, 231.

38. Van Til, *An Introduction to Systematic Theology*, 63.

39. Van Til, *The Doctrine of Scripture* (den Dulk Foundation, 1967), 37; *The Defense of the Faith*, 202; *The Sovereignty of Grace* (Nutley, N. J.: Presbyterian and Reformed, 1969), 63.

40. Van Til, *An Introduction to Systematic Theology*, 139.

41. Van Til, *The Defense of the Faith*, 35.

42. Van Til, *The Theology of James Daane*, 118f.

43. Van Til, *A Christian Theory of Knowledge*, 47.

44. Van Til, *Christianity and Barthianism; The New Modernism.*

doctrine of grace.[45] Secondary causes in the universe have genuine significance "not in spite of, but just because of the fact that they act in accord with the one ultimate *Cause* or plan of God."[46] To summarize and generalize:

> A truly Protestant method of reasoning involves a stress upon the fact that the meaning of every aspect or part of Christian theism depends upon Christian theism as a unit . . . the whole claim of Christian theism is in question in any debate about any fact.[47]

> The starting point, the method, and the conclusion are always involved in one another.[48]

No other American theological writer gives his readers such a profound sense of the *unity* of Christian truth. Again and again we learn that to affirm one doctrine is to affirm another and to affirm the whole; to deny one doctrine is to deny another and to deny the whole. All doctrines are interdependent; the parts depend on the whole; the whole depends on the parts. In this emphasis, Van Til has given Reformed theology much to think about. Any one of the relationships listed above might be made the subject of a theological treatise. Why is it that the self-contained nature of God implies that His revelation be self-attesting? A theologian could spend a great number of pages arguing that point. Van Til himself rarely argues for any of these relationships at any great length. To him they are virtually self-evident. Yet fuller explorations of these matters could bring much edification to the church. How is it, for example, that denial of creation involves denial of God? An answer to that question could help us see the importance of creation in a new way.

Further, the formula "not in spite of, but because of," which recurs so often in Van Til's thought, places a substantial challenge before theologians as they deal with apparent contradictions in biblical teaching. Have we too often been content merely to point out the *consistency* of biblical doctrines when the Bible itself would have us do more? Have we been content merely to show that human responsibility is *compatible with* divine foreordination, rather than showing that human responsibility *depends upon* divine foreordination and is inconceivable without it? If we are going to do the latter, some hard thinking may be necessary. We will certainly have to go beyond the elliptical, highly summarized arguments of Van Til's own writings. Yet the rewards will be great.

---

45. Van Til, *An Introduction to Systematic Theology,* 239; *The Theology of James Daane,* 122.

46. Van Til, *The Defense of the Faith,* 207; cf. 267ff., *Common Grace and the Gospel,* 73, cf. 65ff. As should be evident by now, the formula "not in spite of, but because of" is one of the *leitmotifs* of Van Til's thought.

47. Van Til, *Apologetics,* 73.

48. *Ibid.,* 62.

Van Til's approach here also has another interesting ramification. To-day there is much concern in theology as to the "central focus" of the Christian revelation. Many theologies have arisen attempting to persuade us of the "centrality" of something or other in the Christian faith: theologies of the Word, of "crisis," of personal encounter, of divine acts, of history, of hope, of self-understanding, of celebration, of covenant law, of doxology, and so on. Van Til's emphasis reminds us, however, that *there are many "central" doctrines of the faith,* not just one single one. And further, any scheme which would dismiss *any* teaching of Scripture as unimportant or false must be rejected. *In Christianity, the "central" doctrines do not become central by cancelling out other scriptural teachings; rather, they undergird and support and necessitate those other doctrines.* Though Van Til himself does not say this, his thought suggests the desirability of an orthodox Christian "perspectival" approach to theology: *each major doctrine provides a "perspective" in terms of which the whole of Christianity can be viewed.* The atonement, for example, presupposes certain attributes of God, a certain doctrine of sin, a definite conception of redemptive history; and it in turn generates a further history of redemptive application. The seventh commandment, to use another example, pro-vides a "perspective" upon *all* sin; for idolatry is a form of adultery in Scripture, and idolatry is the essence of sin in general. Thus, all sin is adultery of a sort; and all sin is theft (theft of what is due to God); and all sin is false witness (exchanging the truth of God for a lie). Each of the ten commandments presents a characterization which applies to *all* sin and which therefore defines *all* righteousness. Thus, in Chris-tianity, each major doctrine[49] provides a certain "perspective" upon the *whole* of Christian truth. Each one can be "central." The use of *various* centers at various times can enrich our understanding of Scripture.

II. *Anti-System*

Thus far, I have been intentionally vague as to the precise logical re-lations among Christian doctrines. Van Til's language is not the precise language of a modern logician. One doctrine can "require" or "necessi-tate" another in various ways. To say that one doctrine is true "because" of another is to speak with some ambiguity: even Aristotle recognized four senses of "because." And even when Van Til uses more technical logical terms like "corollary" and "entail," it is not clear that he is using them in their technical senses.

---

49. Even for Van Til, I assume, not all doctrines are "major." "Abraham lived in Ur of the Chaldees" is not as "central" as the doctrine of the Trinity. Yet the line between "major" and "minor" is not sharp, and even "minor" doctrines are systematically related to major ones. Specifically, they presuppose the reliability of Scripture, which in turn presupposes the whole Christian worldview.

One might conclude from what was said above that Van Til regards Christianity as a deductive system in which each doctrine, taken by itself, *logically* implies all the others. Van Til, however, explicitly *denies* this notion. There is no "master concept" from which the whole of Christian doctrine may be logically deduced.[50] But then in what sense is the self-contained character of God "central" to Christianity? In what sense does this doctrine "require" a certain doctrine of Scripture, of Christ, etc.?

Even more perplexing is Van Til's attitude toward the logical consistency of Christian doctrines. We have seen earlier that Van Til affirms the "internal coherence" of the Christian system and attacks positions which introduce contradictions into that system. The natural assumption is that this coherence is a logical coherence. Doesn't he say that "The rules of formal logic must be followed in all our attempts at systematic exposition of God's revelation, whether general or special"?[51] And yet at the same time Van Til teaches that the Christian system is full of "apparent contradictions":

> Now since God is not fully comprehensible to us we are bound to come into what seems to be contradiction in all our knowledge. Our knowledge is analogical and therefore must be paradoxical.[52]

> . . . while we shun as poison the idea of the really contradictory we embrace with passion the idea of the *apparently* contradictory.[53]

All teaching of Scripture is apparently contradictory.[54]

Let us look at some specific examples. With regard to the doctrine of the Trinity, Van Til denies that the paradox of the three and one can be resolved by the formula "one in essence and three in person." Rather, "We do assert that God, that is, the whole Godhead, is one person."[55] Van Til's doctrine, then, can be expressed "One person, three persons"— an apparent contradiction. This is a very bold theological move. Theologians are generally most reluctant to express the paradoxicality of this doctrine so blatantly. Why does Van Til insist on making things so difficult? In the context, he says he adopts this formula to "avoid the specter of brute fact." (Brute fact, in Van Til's terminology, is uninterpreted being.) The argument here is somewhat elliptical, but if we fill in some missing premises, it seems to go like this: If we deny that God is one person,

---

50. Van Til, *The Defense of the Faith*, 205; cf. 227, *A Christian Theory of Knowledge*, 38.

51. Van Til, *Common Grace and the Gospel*, 28. On p. 143 he refers approvingly to Kuyper's view that "all men have to think according to the rules of logic according to which alone the human mind can function." Cf. also references in notes 19-22, above.

52. Van Til, *The Defense of the Faith*, 61.

53. Van Til, *Common Grace and the Gospel*, 9.

54. *Ibid.*, 142.

55. Van Til, *An Introduction to Systematic Theology*, 229.

then the unity among Father, Son, and Holy Spirit becomes an *impersonal* unity. The diversities among the three in that case would not be functions of personal planning and interpretation; rather these diversities would "just happen" to exist. Such a view would in effect place an impersonal "chance" or impersonal "fate" behind and above the persons of the Godhead. Somehow, then, the three persons must function in such *intimate interdependence* that it may be truly said that *the three are one person*.[56] Bold as it may seem, this view not only conforms to the metaphysical teachings implicit in Scripture but also to the simple language by which Scripture refers to God. Scripture, after all, *does* refer to God as one person. It distinguishes among Father, Son, and Holy Spirit; yet very often it speaks of God as a person without mentioning those distinctions. It is true, as the traditional formulae suggest, that God is one in one respect, three in another respect. Such language is necessary to guard against the possibility of a "real contradiction," a chaos, in the Godhead. Yet Scripture does not clearly specify the "respect" in which God is three as over against the "respect" in which God is one. In other words, Scripture leaves us with an "apparent contradiction" here. God is one, and God is three. And Van Til's view gives us an important warning not to go beyond Scripture in this matter.

Van Til treats the relation between God's nature and His attributes in the same way as he treats the trinitarian question: ". . . the unity and the diversity in God are equally basic and mutually dependent upon one another."[57] *God is one and God is many*—that, it seems, is the best we can do. The apparent contradiction might be resolved if we could specify in what respects, precisely, God is one and many, but to do so would be to go beyond Scripture and to raise again "the specter of brute fact." Cosmic impersonalism would again be a threat.

The necessity and freedom of God's will are also paradoxically related according to Van Til. If God's will is directed by His intelligence, then His free acts (creating the world, for example) become necessary: God *had* to create. If, on the other hand, God's free acts are truly free, then it would seem that they must be unconnected with His intelligence and therefore random: God *just happened* to create. Neither alternative is

---

56. The term "person" has a rather different meaning in its modern use from any meaning attached to it (Greek: *hypostasis*) at the time of the Nicene creedal formulation. Van Til's use is more like the modern than like the ancient. Still, it is important to ask about God's "personality" in the modern sense. Scripture does describe God as what *we* would call a "person"—one who thinks, plans, loves, creates, judges, speaks, etc. It is important, then, to ask as Van Til does how "personality" in *this* sense is related to the doctrine of the Trinity. And I believe that Van Til's conclusion is not different from the one we would have to draw with regard to the ancient usage of *hypostasis*.

57. Van Til, *The Defense of the Faith*, 26; cf. *An Introduction to Systematic Theology*, 229.

biblical; nevertheless, Scripture requires us to affirm the intelligence *and* freedom of God's acts. Van Til does suggest that we need to distinguish between two kinds of necessity—the necessity of God's nature and that necessity by which His free acts come about. But, he adds, "this is as far as our finite minds can reach."[58] There is no definitive and final solution for finite thought. Again, the apparent contradiction could be resolved if we could specify the precise differences between the two "necessities," but God has not revealed those differences.

Van Til's paradigm case of the concept of "apparent contradiction" is what he calls the "full-bucket difficulty." *God is self-sufficient;* He needs nothing outside himself; He cannot become greater than He is, in knowledge, love, power, glory, for a greater than God is inconceivable. Nevertheless, *He creates a world for His own glory*—to obtain more glory, to enter into significant knowledge; love- and power-relationships which He would not have entered otherwise. In other words, on the one hand, God's knowledge, love, power, and glory *preclude* addition; on the other hand they *demand* addition.[59] The course of history is somehow significant and important for God, even though that whole course is completely known to God before it begins.[60] Secondary causes are significant and important (again, for God!—God is the determiner of significance), even though God's primary causality controls all that comes to pass.[61] Again, if we could determine more precisely *what sort of* significance world history has for God, then the "contradiction" would drop away. Evidently, there is one sense in which secondary causes *are* "significant" and another sense in which they are *not.* Yet God has not chosen to give us information by which these difficulties might be resolved.

Does God's plan "include" evil? Yes and no. God brings evil to pass, but He is not therefore to be blamed for it. God foreordains sin, but man is not forced to sin. God ordains the damnation of the reprobates, but that gives them no excuse.[62] Apparent contradictions again. But we should note that here, as in the previous cases, Van Til also approves a non-contradictory formulation:

> Thus all Reformed Confessions and all Reformed always reject the *eodem modo* idea. It is abhorrent to any true believer to make God the author of sin, to say that God is as much interested in the

---

58. Van Til, *An Introduction to Systematic Theology,* 249f., cf. 176ff. Note also the reference in note 36 above, where Van Til says that God's will is free *because* it is necessary. Van Til can state that two concepts are "apparently contradictory" while at the same time making the one logically dependent upon the other.

59. Van Til, *Common Grace and the Gospel,* 10; *The Defense of the Faith,* 61f.

60. Van Til, *Common Grace and the Gospel,* 28.

61. *Ibid.,* 73ff., 141ff.; *The Defense of the Faith,* 207ff., 245, 267ff., 269ff.

62. Van Til, *An Introduction to Systematic Theology,* 248; "Nature and Scripture," 271; *Christian-Theistic Ethics,* 36, 139.

death of the sinner as in the blessedness of the saved. God's decree is not *in the same manner* back of reprobation as of election. The counsel of God is *primarily* concerned with the establishment of God's kingdom through Christ. There must be no equal ultimacy of election and reprobation that forgets this fact.[63]

God does not ordain damnation (or, by implication, any other evil) *in the same way* as He ordains good. Somehow the word "ordain" does not designate quite the same sort of divine act in the two cases. Somehow God's plan does not both "include" evil and "exclude" it in the same respect. Yet divine revelation does not tell us precisely in what respect God's plan includes evil and in what respect it excludes it. Thus, a paradox remains for us, though by faith we are confident that there is no paradox for God. Faith is basic to the salvation of our knowledge as well as the salvation of our souls.

In other doctrinal areas also, Van Til formulates his positions in strikingly paradoxical ways. The traditional distinction between the image of God in the "wider" sense (man's personality, moral agency) and the image in the "narrower" sense (knowledge of God, righteousness, holiness) Van Til accepts as only "relatively satisfactory."[64] If pressed, he argues, this distinction would imply that man's personality as created by God has no ethical character—historically a Roman Catholic position rejected by the Reformation.[65] Is it possible, he asks, for the image in the "narrower" sense to be wholly lost in the Fall while the image in the "wider" sense is left entirely intact? Though Van Til does not spell out an alternative view in any precise way, he seems to move in the direction of saying: The image is lost (in some sense) and also remains (in some sense). Since the precise senses are not specified, we are left with a paradoxical formulation. Yet to call such a formulation "contradictory" would be to ignore the fact that specification of the senses is possible in principle, and God is surely capable of specifying them.

Note also: (1) Van Til's view of mankind existing and yet not existing in Adam as its representative;[66] (2) his view that apart from common grace, sin would and would not have destroyed the creative work of God;[67] (3) his view that the unregenerate man is both able and unable to know the truth;[68] (4) his view that the significance of human actions is both guaranteed by, and rendered logically problematic by, the all-controlling

---

63. Van Til, *The Theology of James Daane*, 90.
64. Van Til, *Christian-Theistic Ethics*, 46; cf. *The Defense of the Faith*, 29.
65. Van Til, *Common Grace and the Gospel*, 202ff.
66. Van Til, *The Defense of the Faith*, 249ff.
67. Van Til, *Common Grace and the Gospel*, 199f.
68. Van Til, *An Introduction to Systematic Theology*, 26, 112f.

plan of God;[69] (5) his view of Chalcedon as an acceptance of and formulation of apparently contradictory biblical teaching.[70] In all of these matters, Van Til appears to deny that any fully satisfactory non-paradoxical formulation is possible. Still, in each of these cases (as in the ones discussed more fully in the preceding paragraphs), the "apparent contradiction" appears to arise from our ignorance concerning the precise senses of certain key terms.[71] So construing the problem, it is not difficult for us to assume that the paradoxes are resolvable for one who has more complete or exhaustive knowledge of the truth. Surely we must assume that they are resolvable in God's own thought, and thus not "really" contradictory.

Yet for us men, with the revelation now available to us (which in Van Til's view is sufficient and will not be increased before the return of Christ), the necessity of formulating doctrines in "apparently contradictory" ways certainly increases the difficulty of developing a "system of doctrine," especially a system such as Van Til himself advocates, wherein all doctrines are profoundly interdependent, wherein one doctrine is frequently said to "require" another. How may it be shown that one doctrine "requires" another, when our paradoxical formulations fail even to show how the two are compatible? His stress on apparent contradiction, though it does not render Christianity irrational or illogical, does seem at least to make very difficult if not impossible the task of the systematic theologian. Does this emphasis amount to an anti-system polemic which in effect contradicts his pro-system theme?

III. *The Analogical System*

Van Til reconciles his pro-system statements with his view of "apparent contradiction" by means of his doctrine of analogical reasoning. Only one kind of "system" is possible if we are to be true to God's revelation: an "analogical" system.[72] What does Van Til mean by "analogical system" and "analogical reasoning"?

On first hearing these phrases, we might suppose that Van Til here is advocating a doctrine about Christian religious language—that such language is "analogical," figurative, as opposed to being "literal." The term "analogical" is often used this way in theological and philosophical litera-

---

69. Van Til, *The Theology of James Daane*, 64f.; cf. references in note 46 above. By "logically problematic" I mean that for Van Til the relation of human responsibility to God's plan must invariably be formulated in an "apparently contradictory" fashion.

70. Van Til, *The Defense of the Faith*, 205.

71. Van Til does not himself suggest that the paradoxes turn on such ambiguities; yet all his examples of "apparent contradiction" may be analyzed in such a way.

72. Van Til, *The Doctrine of Scripture*, 123; *A Christian Theory of Knowledge*, 38; *Jerusalem and Athens*, 126.

ture, especially when contrasted with "univocal," as it is in Van Til. It is evident, however, that Van Til's concept of analogy is a doctrine about human reasoning (even human life!) in general, not about religious language in particular. He rarely if ever discusses the religious language question, and he never discusses it in contexts where the concept of "analogy" is prominent. There are two passages in his writings where analogous reasoning is said to legitimize certain "anthropomorphic" expressions.[73] However, in view of Van Til's usual accounts of "analogy" (see below), I would hold that in those two passages, the term "anthropomorphic" means "from a human perspective" in a broad sense, and not the more narrow formulation, "utilizing figures comparing God to man." Van Til may well hold (though he never says so) that since revelation presents God to us "from a human perspective," it often presents God in figurative terms. Yet he has never taught that *all* language about God is figurative, and there is nothing in his thought that demands such a conclusion.

Rather than such a doctrine about language, Van Til's view of analogy is essentially this: analogous reasoning is reasoning which presupposes as its ultimate basis the reality of the biblical God and the authority of His revelation. We shall analyze this concept under three headings: analogy and God, analogy and revelation, analogy and logic.

A. *Analogy and God*

The necessity of reasoning analogically is always implied in the theistic conception of God. If God is to be thought of at all as necessary for man's interpretation of the facts or objects of knowledge, he must be thought of as being determinative of the objects of knowledge. In other words, he must then be thought of as the only ultimate interpreter, and man must be thought of as a finite reinterpreter. Since, then, the absolute self-consciousness of God is the final interpreter of all facts, man's knowledge is analogical of God's knowledge. Since all the finite facts exist by virtue of the interpretation of God, man's interpretation of the finite facts is ultimately dependent upon God's interpretation of the facts. Man cannot, except to his own hurt, look at the facts without looking at God's interpretation of the facts. Man's knowledge of the facts is then a reinterpretation of God's interpretation. It is this that is meant by saying that man's knowledge is analogical of God's knowledge.[74]

Analogical reasoning begins with the assumption that God is both the ultimate *source* of all facts and the ultimate *interpreter* of all facts. Man, therefore, can be "creative" and "interpretative" only in a secondary way. He may create and interpret only that which has *already* been created

---

73. Van Til, *Common Grace and the Gospel*, 73; *A Christian Theory of Knowledge*, 37.

74. Van Til, *A Survey of Christian Epistemology*, 203f.

and interpreted by God. Man does not ultimately determine the nature and meaning of the world; rather, he is born into a world which God has already structured, and he must, willingly or not, live with that God-ordained structure.

Therefore, "God's knowledge is archetypal and ours ectypal."[75] God's thought is "creatively constructive" while ours is "receptively reconstructive."[76] God "interprets absolutely" while man is the "re-interpreter of God's interpretation."[77]

This distinction is both a fact and a norm. It is a *fact,* because human thought *in the nature of the case* can be nothing else than "reinterpretation." It may be a faithful or faithless reinterpretation; it may be a true or false reinterpretation; it may be admittedly reinterpretative or allegedly autonomous; but it cannot help but be reinterpretation, for that is what God made it to be. The distinction is also a *norm:* if our thinking is to be sound and true and right, then it *ought to acknowledge* its character as reinterpretation; it ought to take its actual status as reinterpretation into account; it ought to presuppose that status in all its work. Thus, the fact of our created status entails our obligation to "think as creatures,"[78] to think in a way appropriate to our creaturely status. Analogical reasoning, then, for Van Til, is human thought which is not only reinterpretative (as *all* human thought must be), but which acknowledges its character as re-interpretation and seeks to think in a way appropriate to creatures.

Analogical reasoning, then, is not only dependent upon God, but *self-consciously dependent.* God is not only its creator and sustainer, but also its "ultimate reference point of predication."[79] Analogical reasoning recognizes God as the final authority, the ultimate criterion of truth and falsehood, right and wrong, possibility and impossibility. Our interpretation must be submissive to the authoritative interpretation of God.[80]

This view implies both a continuity and a discontinuity between God's thoughts and those of human analogical reasoning. There is *continuity* because the very nature of analogical reasoning is to agree with God, to conform to God's own thought. But there is also *discontinuity,* for human thought, even analogical human thought, can never be divine. Human thought can never be the ultimate interpretation, the ultimate reference point. Analogical thought, again by its very nature, confesses its creatureli-

---

75. Van Til, *An Introduction to Systematic Theology,* 203. The terminology is from Kuyper's *Encyclopedia.*

76. *Ibid.,* 126.

77. Van Til, *The Defense of the Faith,* 64.

78. Van Til, *Common Grace and the Gospel,* 205.

79. Van Til, *An Introduction to Systematic Theology,* 101.

80. Van Til, *The Doctrine of Scripture,* 15.

ness, its non-divinity. The slogan "thinking God's thoughts after him"[81] reflects both the continuity and the discontinuity: we think God's thoughts (continuity) *after* Him (discontinuity).

Thus, just as it is important for us to *agree* with God, so it is equally important to *distinguish* our thoughts from His. God reveals himself to us, not exhaustively, but "according to man's ability to receive his revelation."[82] We do not know God the same way He knows himself. Without such discontinuity, the continuities mentioned earlier would be meaningless, for if we cannot clearly distinguish between our thoughts and God's, how can we regard the latter as authoritative for the former? Van Til, therefore, even acknowledges a sense in which man himself is a kind of "starting-point" for thought: he is a "proximate" starting-point, while God is the "ultimate" starting-point.[83] God is our final authority; but for that very reason we must be content to think as human beings.

So far, Van Til's position is generally straightforward, and it is hard to see how it could offend any Bible-believing Christian. However, Van Til's view of the continuity and discontinuity between human and divine thought (sketched above) precipitated within Bible-believing Christian circles one of the most heated controversies in Van Til's controversial career—the debate over the "incomprehensibility of God," otherwise known as the "Clark case."[84] In that controversy, the argument focused on Van Til's statement that there is no "identity of content between what God has in his mind and what man has in his mind."[85] As I understand it, this statement is merely another way of asserting the "discontinuity" between divine and human thought which we have discussed above. It sets forth the *same* discontinuity we have already noted, and not some further discontinuity in addition to that one. To deny "identity of content" between God's thought and man's is, for Van Til, simply to assert the Creator-creature distinction in the area of thought. God's concept of a rose, let us say, is different "in content" from man's, because God's concept is the original and ours is derivative; His is self-justifying, while ours must be justified by reference to His. So far as I can see, this is *all* Van Til means to say in denying "identity of content."

I would argue, however (with the benefit of hindsight), that in making

---

81. Van Til uses this slogan: cf. *A Christian Theory of Knowledge*, 16, "Nature and Scripture," 271.

82. Van Til, *A Christian Theory of Knowledge*, 37.

83. Van Til, *An Introduction to Systematic Theology*, 203; cf. *The Doctrine of Scripture*, 14. Cf. also the opening section of Calvin's *Institutes*.

84. The protagonists in the controversy were Van Til and Gordon H. Clark, a well-known Christian apologist and philosopher. I shall not discuss Clark's position, since my purpose is rather to analyze Van Til's.

85. Van Til, *An Introduction to Systematic Theology*, 165; cf. 171ff. Cf. also Van Til, "Introduction" in B. B. Warfield, *The Inspiration and Authority of the Bible*, 33.

such a statement Van Til was somewhat unwise in his choice of terminology. "Content" is an exceedingly ambiguous term when applied to thought. The "content" of my thought may mean (1) my mental images, (2) my beliefs, (3) the things I am thinking of, (4) the epistemological processes by which knowledge is acquired (including the roles of sense-experience, intuition, reason, etc.), (5) the meaning of my language, conceived in abstraction from the linguistic forms used to state that meaning, (6) anything at all to which the physical metaphor "contained in the mind" may conceivably apply. In senses (2) and (3), there seems to be no reason to assert any necessary "difference in content" between divine and human thought. Surely God and man may have the same beliefs and may think about the same things. As for (1) and (4), Scripture tells us very little about the processes of divine thought—how He knows what He knows, whether He has mental images or not, if so what they are like, etc. Doubtless there are continuities and discontinuities in these areas, but the whole question borders on the speculative. As for (5), surely there is an *identity of meaning* between God's words and ours at least on those occasions when God uses human language. Van Til himself, I think, has sense (6) in mind when he denies "identity of content" between divine and human thought. And with that meaning Van Til's assertion is obviously true. There is "in" God's mind what can never be "in" any man's mind, namely, *ultimate authority* and *creative power*. Man can never know fully what it is like to think with such self-validating autonomy. Epistemological lordship attaches to *every* thought God has, and to *no* thought any man ever has. Thus there is, with regard to any item of knowledge, always something "in" God's mind different from anything "in" man's. Yet the preposition "in" here is rather metaphorical, as is the term "content" in sense (6); it is further a rather vague metaphor, one which does not specify with any precision the *sort of* discontinuity Van Til wishes to assert. Still further, it tends to obscure the *continuities* upon which Van Til himself has placed such emphasis—that we must have the *same* opinions God has, that we must think about the *same* matters that God speaks of in His revelation, that we must attach the *same* meanings to God's words that He does, that our thinking must have the same "reference point" God's thinking has (namely, divine authority).[86] To assert without further definition a difference in "content" between divine and human thought obscures the senses in which divine and human thought ought to have the *same* content.[87]

---

86. Van Til, *An Introduction to Systematic Theology*, 165—above the previously cited passage.

87. I might point out another terminological problem which may also have hindered communication during the "Clark case." In my view, it was unfortunate that this controversy was ever described as a controversy over the "incomprehensi-

Whatever we may think about the "content" terminology, however, we cannot deny the basic points Van Til is making here about analogical reasoning: (1) our thought must *conform* to God's, His thought being the ultimate standard of truth; and (2) we must *not confuse* our thought with God's, for ours is *not* ultimate, *not* self-validating.

B. *Analogy and Revelation*

If analogous reasoning means bringing our creaturely thoughts into accord with (but not into identity with) God's divine thoughts, how is this to be done? Certainly not by direct inspection of the divine thought-processes, as if I could distinguish an apple from a tomato by comparing them with duplicates in God's mind.[88] That sort of Platonism is far from Van Til's position. Van Til rather affirms with all Reformed thought that we can have *no* knowledge of God unless He *voluntarily* reveals himself. Our only access to God's mind is through His voluntary self-revelation—His word. Thus, Van Til is able to define analogical reasoning as reasoning which is fully subject to God's authoritative word.[89] This revelation is not exhaustive, and therefore *analogical reasoning may not attain to exhaustive knowledge.*[90]

Van Til's doctrine of revelation is for the most part standard, familiar, Reformed theology. *General revelation* in his view is revelation given by God to all men through nature and through human constitution, declaring the reality and nature of God, and revealing enough of God's will for man as to leave sinners without excuse (Ps. 19:1ff.; Rom. 1–2). *Special revelation* consists in the words spoken by God to and through prophets, apostles, the incarnate Christ, and the written Scripture, not only once again to display His nature and utter His commands, but particularly to set forth His provision for the forgiveness of sin in the work of Christ.

What is unusual about Van Til's teaching in this area, however, is (a) his emphasis on the correlativity between general and special reve-

---

bility of God." The term "incomprehensibility" generally denotes a relation between human knowledge and the *being* of God, not a relation between human knowledge and divine knowledge. To say that God is incomprehensible is generally to say that we lack exhaustive knowledge of God's *being,* of what he *is* (and does). In the Clark controversy, however, the term was often used, as we have seen, to denote various sorts of discontinuities between our *knowledge* (of anything) and God's *knowledge* (of anything), or between our thoughts and his thoughts. Doubtless the two problems are closely related. The discrepancies between human and divine thoughts certainly account at least in part for the limitations in our knowledge of God's being. Yet in my view the two problems should have been more clearly distinguished than such use of "incomprehensible" permits them to be.

88. Cf. Van Til, *The Defense of the Faith,* 300f.

89. Van Til, *Common Grace and the Gospel,* 206; *An Introduction to Systematic Theology,* 256–60; *Jerusalem and Athens,* 126; cf. "Introduction," 49.

90. Van Til, *A Christian Theory of Knowledge,* 16.

lation and (b) the delicate balance he strikes between this correlativity and the primacy of Scripture.

(1) *The Correlativity of General and Special Revelation:* Van Til likes to emphasize that general and special revelation are related to one another in "organic, supplemental fashion."[91] By this he means, *first,* that neither has ever existed apart from the other. Even before the Fall, from the first moment of man's existence, he was confronted *both* with God's spoken word (Gen. 1:28f.; 2:16f.) *and* with God's revelation in creation. *Second,* neither was ever intended to function apart from the other. Fact-revelation and word-revelation "require each other."[92] The fact always "needed to be explained by God himself,"[93] and the word always explains *facts* about God, man, nature, and redemptive history. Either without the other would be unintelligible, would communicate nothing. Adam needed to hear a word of God to know his duty with respect to the trees of the garden, but this verbal command presupposes Adam's knowledge of the "situation": "The supernatural could not be recognized for what it was unless the natural were also recognized for what it was."[94] *Third,* both general revelation and special revelation are "necessary, authoritative, clear and sufficient." Those four adjectives apply to general revelation in view of its distinctive purpose. To *render sinners without excuse* and to *provide the factual referent* for special revelation, general revelation is necessary, speaks with authority, speaks clearly, and contains sufficient content to accomplish its work.[95]

This sort of emphasis is unusual in American theology, though it has precedents in the Dutch literature. I find it refreshing and exciting; its implications for theological work are innumerable. For one thing, it means that we need not be embarrassed about using *extra-scriptural information* to interpret Scripture. If indeed the creation were somehow autonomous, then we might fear that the use of such data might to some extent hide the full truth of God's revelation. But creation is not independent of God.[96] God controls it and speaks through all of it. And He has chosen to reveal himself, not by nature or Scripture alone, but always by the two together in organic union. Thus, we can use such data fearlessly and thankfully.

---

91. Van Til, *The Doctrine of Scripture,* 65.

92. Van Til, "Introduction," 32.

93. Van Til, *An Introduction to Systematic Theology,* 133.

94. Van Til, *Apologetics,* 30.

95. Van Til, "Nature and Scripture," 269ff.; *Apologetics,* 30ff.

96. Notice that Van Til's doctrine of Scripture is distinctively *Calvinistic.* It presupposes an uncompromising view of God's sovereignty. Van Til is fond of speaking about the "isolation of the Reformed view of Scripture" (cf. *The Doctrine of Scripture,* 37). The division between Calvinism and Arminianism is not only over soteriology and providence, but it cuts across the whole range of Christian doctrine, in Van Til's view.

For another thing, Van Til's emphasis frees us to see a very important principle: Scripture is seen for what it is *only* when it is properly related to the world into which it has come. God never intended otherwise. This means not only that Scripture must be interpreted in the light of its original cultural environment, but also that it must be *applied* to our own lives and culture—to the environment in which it *now* speaks. We do not know what Scripture says until we know how it relates to our world. *The question of interpretation and the question of application are the same.* To ask what Scripture says, or what it means, is always to ask a question about application. A question about the meaning of Scripture always arises out of a personal problem—an inability to relate the words of Scripture to our lives, to our language, our thought-forms, our culture, our fears and hopes.

This principle, in turn, helps us attain greater clarity on the question of what theology is all about. *Theology is simply the application of Scripture to all areas of human life.* On this matter, Reformed writers have often been unhelpful. They have talked about theology as a study of God or Scripture, as an ordering of biblical data, as a process of theory construction from the facts of the Bible, etc. But they have not seriously asked the question, "Why do we need theology if Scripture is sufficient?" Often they have talked as if theology is necessary for us to obtain the truth about God, forgetting for the moment that God has *already* told us the truth about himself in Scripture. Sometimes they have suggested that the scriptural account of the truth is somehow defective—in form if not in content—and that theology is needed to remedy that defect, to put the Scripture into proper form, perhaps. Such options are not open to a follower of Van Til. *Scripture is not lacking in truth, order, rationality.* It is not a brute fact which stands only as data for human interpretation. It *is* interpretation—divine interpretation. We need theology not because of any defect in Scripture, but because of *defects in us,* because of our inability to *relate* the clear revelation of Scripture to our own lives. We need theology—not to restructure or improve upon Scripture, but to *apply* Scripture to our lives.[97]

If theology is "application," then theology necessarily must make use of general as well as special revelation. To know how Scripture *applies,* we must know something about ourselves and our world. If we are to know how Scripture applies to abortions and ecology and energy crises and nuclear war, we must have at our disposal more than the text of

---

97. Van Til himself has not defined theology as "application" as we have in this paragraph. His own definitions of theology are of a more traditional sort. But this is one of those areas where we must go beyond Van Til in order to be fully true to his distinctive insights. The concept of theology as "application" has a firm basis in the thought of Van Til, though it is not found among his explicit doctrines.

Scripture; we must have information about all these matters as well. But if Van Til is right, we may use such information without embarrassment.

(2) *The Primacy of Scripture:* But what has happened to the sufficiency of Scripture in all of this? If theology may and must use general revelation "without embarrassment," and if general revelation is needed for us to understand (= apply) Scripture, then in what sense does Scripture have primacy? If our knowledge of Scripture is dependent to some extent upon our "natural knowledge," can we have any more confidence in Scripture than we can have in our natural knowledge? Does Scripture itself, on this view, merely become another form of general revelation?

We have already observed that for Van Til nature and Scripture are related in "organic, supplemental fashion."[91] *Scripture is unintelligible without those facts which it interprets, but the facts also are unintelligible apart from God's spoken and written interpretation of them.* Even before the Fall, therefore, there is a sense in which God's spoken words had a "priority" over His revelation in nature. Man was to accept God's spoken words as ultimately authoritative interpretation, as that interpretation by which all other interpretation must be judged. Eve sinned in accepting the serpent's words (and eventually her own) as having this ultimate authority. It was not that God's spoken words were more true or more authoritative than His revelation in nature. Rather, God's spoken words were more authoritative than any human (or Satanic) *interpretation* of natural revelation. Thus, Adam and Eve were under obligation to make God's *spoken* words the "starting point" of their thought, to accept them as the criterion for all sound interpretation of God's world.

After the Fall, the spoken and written words of God take on an even more crucial role, since man's normal activity of interpreting the universe has been distorted by sin.[98] After the Fall, it becomes even more important to point to these spoken and written words as the only ultimately authoritative sentences known to man. Therefore, "the revelation in Scripture must be made our starting-point. It is only in the light of the Protestant doctrine of Scripture that one can obtain also Protestant doctrine of the revelation of God in nature."[99] "But since the entrance of sin it is necessary to begin even the study of the works of God through the Word of God."[100]

The point is that natural revelation must indeed be used in the interpretation (= application) of Scripture, but once that interpretation is ascer-

---

98. Van Til, *A Christian Theory of Knowledge,* 163f.; "Introduction," 33; *An Introduction to Systematic Theology,* 110f.

99. Van Til, *Apologetics,* 27.

100. Van Til, *The Doctrine of Scripture,* 120; cf. "Nature and Scripture," 265; *Christian-Theistic Ethics,* 133, 139f.

tained, it must take precedence over hypotheses derived from *any* other source. "Theology as application" presupposes a finished, complete, authoritative Scripture (see above discussion). Theology is the application of *Scripture* and Scripture alone.[101] Even when we use extra-scriptural information (as we must) to understand Scripture, we must hold *loosely* to this information—loosely enough to allow Scripture to call it in question. It is only when our methods of Scripture interpretation are themselves purified by Scripture that real progress can be made in theology.

In Van Til's view, the primacy of Scripture is comprehensive—it covers all areas of life. He clearly rejects the view that the Bible contains only "truths of faith" or "religious teaching" as over against, say, teaching about the physical universe.[102] The philosopher, too, is "directly subject to the Bible. . . ."[103] Directly or indirectly, there is no matter about which the Bible is silent.[104]

It has been asked that if Scripture has such primacy for Van Til, why is his method not more "exegetical"? G. C. Berkouwer has chastened Van Til on this score, and Van Til himself has admitted guilt in this regard.[105] Van Til rarely exegetes specific biblical passages; his terminology is often abstract and philosophical. There is some truth in this criticism, but there is also much to be said in favor of Van Til's approach. *First,* many critics are unaware of the extent to which Van Til's mind is steeped in the content of Scripture. His sermons and class lectures are full of biblical references, allusions, illustrations. For some reason, this emphasis has not been prominent in his published works; yet his published works grow out of this Bible-saturated mentality. *Second,* many critics are unaware of the fact that Van Til's favorite professor at Princeton was Geerhardus Vos, the brilliant biblical theologian. The influence of Vos upon Van Til is profound, though rarely seen on the surface of Van Til's writings. There are places in Van Til's works, however, where the influence of Vos

101. Nothing could be further from Van Til's view than the idea that nature-study reveals divine commandments beyond Scripture and equal to Scripture in authority. Van Til's *sola scriptura* stands in sharp contrast to the views of Dooyeweerd and his followers. See my article, "Toronto, Reformed Orthodoxy and the Word of God," *Vanguard* (Jan.–Feb., 1975) and my pamphlet (with L. J. Coppes), *The Amsterdam Philosophy* (Phillipsburg, N. J.: Harmony Press, 1972).

102. Van Til, "Bavinck the Theologian," 10; *Apologetics,* 2; *The Defense of the Faith,* 24; cf. *The Doctrine of Scripture,* 89ff. Compare this with the assertion of Dooyeweerd that Scripture is a "book of faith" and therefore may not speak, e.g., of the chronology of creation: Dooyeweerd, *In the Twilight of Western Thought* (Nutley, N. J.: Craig Press, 1968), 149ff.

103. Van Til, *Apologetics,* 37. Cf. the discussion in *Jerusalem and Athens,* 81, in which Dooyeweerd takes issue with Van Til's position on this point.

104. Van Til, *Apologetics,* 2, *The Defense of the Faith,* 24.

105. Van Til, *Jerusalem and Athens,* 203f.; cf. *Toward a Reformed Apologetics* (no publication data), 27.

is unmistakable to anyone who reflects on the matter.[106] *Third,* Van Til has had the advantage of teaching at an institution where there has been a remarkable unity of mind among the faculty. Unlike some theologians, Van Til has felt that he could *trust* his colleagues in the exegetical disciplines and build upon their exegetical work. Van Til's trust in his colleagues has given him the freedom to concentrate his work in areas most suited to his own gifts, which are more philosophical than philological. Thus in reply to Berkouwer's criticism, he simply refers to the exegetical work of John Murray as expressing his own view. *Finally,* we must rethink, in my view, our common concept of what "exegesis" is. If, as we have argued earlier, *interpretation and application of Scripture are the same thing,* then we ought to conclude that *"exegesis" is a broader discipline* than it is often conceived to be. Is Van Til not doing "exegesis" when he translates the biblical concepts into philosophical language?[107] What is the difference, really, between translating biblical concepts into philosophic terms and translating Greek words into English? The two activities require different sorts of skills, but is it really fair to describe the one activity as "exegetical" and to deny such a description to the other? Is Van Til not doing "exegesis" when he applies biblical teachings to problems of philosophy and apologetics? What is the difference, really, between applications of that sort and applications to problems of achieving syntactical equivalence? Perhaps when all is said and done it will be seen that Van Til's work is indeed "exegetical" in a very significant sense. This is not to reject the need or importance of those grammatical and historical studies which are commonly called "exegesis." These considerations do suggest, however, that the *whole* work of exegesis cannot be done by any one man, by any one method, by any one set of gifts.

C. *Analogy and Logic*

But I seem to have forgotten the problem which led me to consider Van Til's concept of "analogical reasoning" in the first place. How do we reconcile Van Til's emphasis on "system" with his zest for "paradox"? How is it that the doctrines of Christianity are both *dependent* on one another and somehow in *tension* with one another? Our earlier discussion of analogical reasoning is not irrelevant to this point. We have learned that analogical reasoning is the first kind of "thinking God's thoughts after him"—a type of thinking which seeks *conformity to God's thoughts* while

---

106. Note particularly the emphasis on "taking history seriously" in *Common Grace and the Gospel* (*passim*), the discussion of the kingdom of God in *Christian-Theistic Ethics,* the frequent references to the "Adamic consciousness," etc., as in *An Introduction to Systematic Theology,* 25ff., and the discussion of modern trends in terms of God's covenants with Adam, Noah, Abraham, etc., in *The Great Debate Today* (Nutley, N. J.: Presbyterian and Reformed, 1971).

107. Cf. Van Til, *The Defense of the Faith,* 40n.

simultaneously acknowledging its own *creatureliness*. We have learned that analogical reasoning, therefore, is reasoning which is subject to God's revelation in general and which tests all ideas by the criterion of Scripture. As such, this reasoning attains truth, but not all the truth. It is true as far as it goes, but not exhaustive. It is true insofar as it actually conforms to God's mind, but the *amount of truth obtainable is limited* by (a) the creaturely status of the reasoner, and (b) the sovereign decision of God concerning what is to be revealed and what kept secret.

Insofar as we attain truth, we attain a sense of the *interconnectedness of the creation*. God's plan is a wise one. He has not planned any one thing in creation without taking everything else into account. All elements of His plan "dovetail" with one another. Scripture often reflects upon these interconnections: faith establishes the law (Rom. 3:31); the glorification of the elect necessitated the sufferings of Christ (Heb. 2:10); true faith always issues in good works (James 2:18); to control the tongue is to control the whole body (James 3:2); to disobey one point of the law is to be guilty of all (James 2:10). A truly biblical theology will reflect upon these interconnections, for they are part of God's truth.

Since, however, *our knowledge is limited* both by our created status and by God's sovereign limitation of revelation, we can expect to find paradox also in Scripture. If we do not know *all* the truth, then we do not know *all* the interconnections between the truths. And *paradox,* as we have earlier presented it, is simply *the result of our ignorance about interconnections.* In many doctrinal areas, we do not know fully *how* various elements of God's plan are related to one another. We do not know precisely *how* they "dovetail," *how* they take account of one another. We know that they *do* dovetail, for we know that God's plan is wise and exhaustive, and usually we know how they fit together to some degree, but the gaps in our knowledge often demand that we rest content with a paradoxical formulation.

God is good, yet He foreordains evil deeds. We know that these truths are compatible, for Scripture teaches both and God does not deny himself. We know, further, that the denial of any one may lead to the denial of the other, and in that sense the two truths are "interdependent." God can foreordain evil only if He is himself good, for in Scripture "evil" is "evil" only by contrast with the goodness of God. God is truly good only if the evil in the world is foreordained by Him, for only if evil is fully controlled by God can we be confident that there is a good purpose in it, and only if there is a good purpose in it can we trust the overall good purpose of God. Scripture, then, teaches us that these two truths are interdependent; they "require" each other. Yet at the same time there is paradox here. Indeed, in this case we know not only *that* there is interdependence, but we also know, to some extent, *how* there is interdependence. But we do not have the *full* knowledge of the "how." There is still something strange about this, something we cannot quite reconcile. How *can* a good God foreordain evil? Thus, we are in a strange state of affairs: we have two propositions ("God is good" and "God foreordains evil") which we can show to be *logically interdependent* in one sense; yet we *cannot* show them to be *logically compatible* except by an appeal to faith! Strange indeed; yet this is where we must stand if we are to do justice both to the truth of God's revelation and to the limitations of our creaturely knowledge, if we are to "reason analogically." This *balance of interdependence and paradox* is in the interest of thinking in submission to Scripture. Scripture must be followed both in its assertions of interdependence and in its refusal to reconcile all doctrines to our satisfaction.

But to what extent, then, may we use *logic* in the derivation of "good and necessary consequences" from Scripture? Are we to deduce doctrines from one another only when Scripture itself does that explicitly? Or may we go beyond what Scripture teaches explicitly to unfold its *implicit* message? Surely Van Til thinks we can. But to what extent? How?

Van Til's general teaching on logic is along the following lines:[108] The *validity of the laws of logic* derives from the *character of God*.[109] God is not subject to some source of (logical or other) possibility more ultimate than himself.[110] Rather, He *himself alone determines ultimately what is possible*.[111] It is God, therefore, who both vindicates and limits the competence of human logic. First, He *vindicates* it. His revelation contains no logical contradiction—no "real" contradiction. There are *apparent* contradictions in Scripture, but *only* apparent ones.[112] Apparent to whom? They appear ultimately irreconcilable to unbelievers because unbelievers have a false view of the foundation of logic.[113] But the "ap-

---

108. Van Til's idealist philosophical training creates some problems in assessing his view of logic. It is not always clear when he is using the term "logic" to mean *formal logic* and when he is using it (as in idealism) to refer to the *methodology of thought in general*. In my discussion, formal logic is in view throughout, and I have tried to set forth Van Til's views on that narrow subject. I may not always have been successful, but rather often the distinction is not important, since Van Til's views on formal logic often parallel closely his views of intellectual methodology in general.

109. Van Til, *A Christian Theory of Knowledge*, 202; *An Introduction to Systematic Theology*, 11, 37, 256; *The Doctrine of Scripture*, 72, *Common Grace and the Gospel*, 28.

110. Van Til, *A Christian Theory of Knowledge*, 202; *An Introduction to Systematic Theology*, 11.

111. Van Til, *The Doctrine of Scripture*, 131.

112. Van Til, *The Defense of the Faith*, 61f.; *A Christian Theory of Knowledge*, 38.

113. Van Til, *Common Grace and the Gospel*, 28; *The Defense of the Faith*, 253; *An Introduction to Systematic Theology*, 171, 230. Van Til grants that unbeliever and believer may observe the same laws of formal logic: *An Introduction to Systematic Theology*, 37, 254; *The Defense of the Faith*, 296ff.; *Common Grace and the Gospel*, 27. The difference is that believer and unbeliever disagree on the

parent contradictions" also are apparent to all men, believers and unbelievers alike, because of their *finitude*.[114] Still, from God's point of view,
there is no contradiction; and thus the believer knows that whatever may
seem to be the case, God's revelation is fully consistent with itself. Logic
applied to God's revelation, therefore, will not lead us astray, if it is *used*
rightly. Logic itself, properly used, will discover no real contradiction in
Scripture.

Second, "proper use" involves certain *limitations* in the process of logical reasoning. We cannot reason any way we want to. We must reason
in full awareness of the fact that God is the foundation of logic.[115] Logic
itself does not determine what is possible or probable; only God does
that.[116] Logic does not give to man exhaustive knowledge; only God
has that.[117] Thus, we cannot assume that all biblical doctrines can be
shown to be fully consistent in terms of our present understanding.[118]
Van Til says, therefore, that the "system" of Christian theology is not a
"deductive" system, and that we must not use "deductive" exegesis.[119]
What does Van Til mean by "deductive" here? He does not actually
define the term anywhere, perhaps assuming (I think wrongly) that it
needs no explanation. Judging from his overall position, however, I
would say that in opposing "deductivism" he means to say (1) that
theology ought not to make deductions from one or several doctrines,
the conclusions of which contradict other scriptural teachings;[120] (2) that
theology ought not to assume that it can demonstrate the formal logical
consistency of all its doctrines (see above discussion); and (3) that there-

---

basis of logic and that they hold different "premises" about ultimate origins and
authority. Cf. *Apologetics*, 50; *A Survey of Christian Epistemology*, 213f.

114. Van Til, *The Defense of the Faith*, 228. Van Til leaves open (as he must, to
avoid speculation) the question of *how* God resolves these apparent contradictions,
whether by a better-than-human logic, by fuller knowledge of the facts, or by somehow transcending the whole logic/fact problematic.

115. Van Til, *An Introduction to Systematic Theology*, 11; *Common Grace and
the Gospel*, 28. Van Til criticizes Hodge, not for using logical reasoning to evaluate
Scripture, but rather for failing adequately to distinguish Christian from non-
Christian *ways* of doing so: *An Introduction to Systematic Theology*, 31ff.; *Apologetics*, 47ff.

116. Van Til, *An Introduction to Systematic Theology*, 256; *Jerusalem and
Athens*, 19; *Common Grace and the Gospel*, 28.

117. Van Til, *A Christian Theory of Knowledge*, 37f.; *The Defense of the Faith*,
228.

118. Van Til, *An Introduction to Systematic Theology*, 169ff.; *Common Grace
and the Gospel*, 10. In the latter passage he suggests that the contradiction appears
only at "first sight." Elsewhere, he seems to argue that it is irresolvable by any
created intellect.

119. Van Til, *A Christian Theory of Knowledge*, 38; *The Defense of the Faith*,
204f., 227; *The Doctrine of Scripture*, 123; *An Introduction to Systematic Theology*,
257; *Common Grace and the Gospel*, 202.

120. Above references (previous note). Also cf. Van Til, *An Introduction to
Systematic Theology*, 256; *Jerusalem and Athens*, 126.

fore the *characteristic method of theology* is not deduction (as in Euclid's geometry) but rather a *putting together of all the biblical data on a particular subject,* adopting paradoxical formulations when these are warranted by the biblical teaching. In this way we should understand the more obscure formulations of Van Til's method, for example, that "we seek to *implicate* ourselves more deeply into a comprehension of God's plan,"[121] and that "it is reasoning in a spiral fashion rather than in a linear fashion."[122]

For all of this it must be admitted that there remains some unclarity in Van Til's teaching about logic, for he does not always explain adequately why he uses deductions in some cases and rejects them in others. For instance, Van Til admits that there *is* a proper use for logical deduction in theology, despite the above-mentioned limitations.[123] As over against the Lutheran, Pieper, Van Til insists that "God can reveal only that which is consistent with his nature as a self-contained being."[124] He argues that it is irrationalism to say that "God is both omnipotent and not omnipotent."[124] He denies that "the Bible can teach both that God elects men to salvation and at the same time that they have the power to reject the grace of God."[125] In these cases, he is deducing (logically! how else?) from one scriptural truth the negation of its opposite. He is saying that since Scripture teaches a particular truth, it cannot (logically) teach the opposite of that truth. On the other hand, he forbids us to "start with the idea of the sovereign control of God over all things and deduce from it the idea that there is no human responsibility."[125] In the one case, logical deduction is permitted, even demanded. In the other case, it is forbidden. Yet in this context, Van Til does not state clearly how the cases differ. Is it that the one sort of deduction is formally valid and the other one is not? Is it that one deduction takes account of all scriptural data while the other does not? Van Til does not say.

Further: to say that God is both omnipotent and not omnipotent is indeed to say something "apparently contradictory." It may be "really contradictory." But, of course, if "omnipotent" and "not omnipotent" employ different senses of "omnipotent," then this apparent contradiction is biblically resolvable. Yet Van Til's argument suggests that in *this* case (though not in others) we *know* that the contradiction is a real one (not merely "apparent"), and therefore we must reject it. But *how* do we know that *this* contradiction is "real" while others are only "apparent"? *How*

---

121. Van Til, *A Survey of Christian Epistemology,* 7.

122. *Ibid.,* 201. Van Til sometimes uses the phrase "circular reasoning," but "spiral reasoning" is far closer to the concept he seeks to convey.

123. *Ibid.,* 7.

124. Van Til, *A Christian Theory of Knowledge,* 202.

125. *Ibid.,* 38. Cf. references above, notes 19-22.

do we know that one contradiction is irresolvable while another is resolvable, when we cannot ourselves resolve either one?

Van Til does explain why we must sometimes be satisfied with apparently contradictory formulations. He does not explain why in *some* cases we must rest content with such paradox while in *other* cases (as in the Pieper example) we must press for an explicit logical consistency. I suspect, however, that if Van Til were to address this problem, he would do it somewhat as follows: Since we believe that there is no "real" contradiction in Scripture, our exegesis should strive to achieve, as much as is humanly possible, a logically consistent interpretation of biblical teaching. Yet this goal is not the primary goal. *The primary goal of exegesis is not logical consistency but faithfulness to the text.* And sometimes in trying to formulate one doctrine with logical consistency, we may find ourselves compromising another doctrine of Scripture. When that happens, something is wrong. *We must not simply push our logic relentlessly to the point where we ignore or deny a genuine biblical teaching.* Rather, we must rethink our whole procedure—our exegesis, our reasoning, the extra-biblical knowledge we bring to bear on the matter, etc. *If no explicit logical consistency can be obtained without conflict with other biblical teaching, then we must remain satisfied with paradox.* In the omnipotence example, explicit logical consistency is possible without any compromise of biblical teaching. Scripture teaches that God is omnipotent. It does not teach the opposite. Logically consistent affirmation of God's omnipotence does not put us in conflict with any other biblical teaching. Therefore we affirm it and insist upon logical consistency. In the example of God's sovereignty and human responsibility, the case is somewhat different. Here there is (in Van Til's mind) an "apparent contradiction." Yet to remove that contradiction would be to compromise either God's sovereignty or man's responsibility. That may not be done, since both doctrines are clearly taught in Scripture. The general principle: we may (and ought to) use logical deduction freely except where such deduction puts us in conflict with the explicit teachings of Scripture.

But if this is the proper analysis of Van Til's position, what are we to make of his statement that "All teaching of Scripture is apparently contradictory"?[126] This statement is rather strange since, as we have seen above, Van Til sometimes *refuses* to accept "apparently contradictory" formulations of scriptural teaching. The omnipotence of God, for Van Til, is *not* (it would seem) an "apparently contradictory" doctrine. It is *wrong,* in his estimation, to say that God both is and is not omnipotent. Furthermore, as we have seen earlier, Van Til does approve other formulations which are not in any sense "apparently contradictory." When he

---

126. Van Til, *Common Grace and the Gospel,* 142.

says, then, that "all teaching of Scripture is apparently contradictory," we are tempted to think that here (as elsewhere; see above, note 108) Van Til has something other than formal logic in mind. Indeed, the paragraph which explains this statement makes no mention of formal contradiction or even of formal logic in general. It simply presents the sovereignty and authority of God over our thought. Is "apparent contradiction" here just a metaphor for the general subordination of man's thought to God's?

A metaphor, perhaps, but not "just" a metaphor. At this point it is important for us to note Van Til's view of Christian doctrines as "limiting" "supplementative" concepts. This principle is the connecting link, in a sense, between Van Til's general view of analogical reasoning and his specific view of formal logic. In saying that *theological concepts are "limiting concepts,"* Van Til is drawing out an *implication of man's creaturely status.* Since man is finite, none of his concepts exhausts the "essence of the thing it seeks to express."[127] Our concept of a tree may be accurate as far as it goes, but it can never *exhaustively* describe the tree. The same holds true for our concepts of God, sin, salvation, etc. Even the concepts of Scripture, presented as they are in human language and adapted therefore to human understanding, do not *exhaustively* describe the realities to which they refer. Scripture tells us what we need to know, but it does not tell us everything. Our concepts, therefore, are "approximations" to the truth in a certain sense.[128] Caution is needed here. Van Til is not saying, for example, that the doctrine of justification by faith is only "approximately true" in the sense of being partly false. Rather, this and other biblical doctrines are completely and dependably true, yet they do not tell us everything God knows about the matters in question. The fact that all doctrines are "non-exhaustive" in this sense implies that various doctrines should be seen as "supplementary" to one another.[129] Scripture clearly

---

127. *Ibid.,* 201. Cf. Van Til, *An Introduction to Systematic Theology,* 256. The term "limiting concept" comes from the philosophy of Immanuel Kant. Kant argued that the "noumenal world," the world as it really is, could not be known by man, but that the *idea* of a noumenal world could be entertained and used for a certain purpose: "The concept of a noumenon is thus a merely *limiting concept,* the function of which is to curb the pretensions of sensibility; and it is therefore only of negative employment." Kant, *Critique of Pure Reason,* tr. Norman Kemp Smith (New York: St. Martin's Press, 1929), 272. In Kant's thought, a "limiting concept" has no positive content. For Kant, "God" is a limiting concept, and this means, not that God actually exists, but only that the term "God" may properly be used in describing the limitedness of our experience. To say that "God exists," for Kant, means only that our experience is limited *as if* by God. Van Til, however, uses the term very differently. In his thought, limiting concepts *do* have positive significance. God really *does* exist, though our concept of God is a "limiting concept." To say that the concept of God is a "limiting concept" in Van Til's thought is merely to say that our knowledge of who God is, though true, is non-exhaustive.

128. *Ibid.,* 11.

129. Van Til, *An Introduction to Systematic Theology,* 255ff.

teaches that God is sovereign, but it does not tell us in complete (exhaustive) detail how His sovereignty operates. The theological concept "divine sovereignty" does not suffice to comprehend and exhaust all of God's actual relations to the world. Thus, we ought not to derive our view of human responsibility exclusively from our concept of divine sovereignty, while ignoring what Scripture explicitly says about human responsibility. We should rather allow the two concepts to supplement one another: the biblical teaching on human responsibility will deepen our understanding of divine sovereignty, and vice versa. If putting the two together produces an "apparent contradiction," then so be it. But even the recognition of logical tension helps the believer to see the deeper logical unity of the two doctrines. For the sovereignty of God cannot be seen for what it is—that is, in its full paradoxicality!—except in its relationship to human responsibility. It is in this sort of way that Van Til can describe the two doctrines as "requiring one another" while at the same time insisting that their relationship is "apparently contradictory."

But remember that *all* teachings of Scripture are "limiting concepts." *All* concepts of Scripture are "mutually supplementative" in the above sense. The doctrine of justification by faith also supplements, and is supplemented by, the doctrine of divine sovereignty. The doctrine of divine sovereignty tells us what sort of God is justifying us. Thus, the doctrine of justification by faith incorporates the paradox of divine sovereignty. The doctrine of justification by faith—when fully explained in its relations to the rest of scriptural truth—is just as paradoxical as divine sovereignty. Even the omnipotence of God, then, shares with other doctrines a paradoxical element. That paradoxical element is not properly (scripturally) formulated by the phrase "God is and is not omnipotent." We reject, on scriptural authority, *that* paradox. Yet there is another sort of paradox which applies to the divine omnipotence. The omnipotence of God is "limited" in a sense. God cannot do "everything" if that "everything" includes things contrary to His nature or contrary to His promises, or contrary to His eternal purpose. God's "omnipotence" will not rob man of his responsibility, nor will it eliminate the significance of human action as a secondary cause.

"Apparent contradiction," then, results from the "limiting" nature of biblical concepts. And since these "limiting concepts" are "supplementative," the paradoxes which attach to one attach to all, while at the same time each concept is seen to "require" all the rest. This does not mean that *every* paradox is to be accepted simply because it is a paradox. The paradoxes must be exegetically formulated. Nor does it mean that every doctrine must always be stated in paradoxical terminology. Yet the paradoxes found in Scripture must be fearlessly stated in any complete theological work, and the relations of these paradoxes to each biblical doctrine must be traced. There is a sense, then, in which "all teaching of Scripture is apparently contradictory": (a) all teachings of Scripture are "limiting concepts"; (b) limiting concepts generate apparent contradictions; (c) since limiting concepts are supplementative, an apparent contradiction in one doctrine generates apparent contradictions in all doctrines.

Does this doctrine render Scripture unintelligible? If all doctrines are apparently contradictory, do they have any meaning at all? It is not enough to reply that the contradictions are "apparent" though not "real." An "apparent contradiction," before it is resolved, poses the same problems of intelligibility as a "real contradiction," it would seem. Or does it? Let us go back to our earlier remarks about "theology as application." If interpretation and application are the same, then *the question of intelligibility becomes the question of whether a consistent pattern of application is possible*. A sentence may be intelligible, even though it does not conform to logical canons, if it unambiguously dictates a particular response on the part of the reader or hearer. In a sense, logical laws themselves are secondary to "intelligibility" in this broad sense. Logic aims (fallibly) to describe the conditions under which such application is possible. But as many contemporary logicians have observed, no present logical system describes *all* such conditions of intelligibility. Logic has made only small steps in this task, describing the conditions of intelligibility for a few key terms like "all," "if-then," "some," "none," etc. It has succeeded in analyzing these key terms only in certain narrowly defined contexts of their occurrence. Now, since scriptural doctrines are not "really" contradictory, they are intelligible, but their intelligibility is not demonstrable by the limited canons of current human logic. For example, according to Van Til, man has (in one sense) and has not (in another) lost the image of God as a result of the Fall. Since the senses are not clearly specifiable, we have apparent contradiction, but since God knows what the senses are, there is no real contradiction. Is this doctrine intelligible? Yes, for as taught in Scripture it has a clear application. We are to treat men as made in the image of God, even though they are fallen (Gen. 9:6; James 3:9). We have no right to despise our fellow men on the ground that they have lost the image of God. Though the supposed right to despise our fellow men might seem to follow from part of the doctrine taken in isolation, it is a conclusion uniformly—consistently!—rejected by Scripture. The "loss" of the image *does* have a legitimate application, but not an application contrary to that of the "continuance" of the image. The "loss" of the image motivates us to recognize our own need for renewal, the need to "put on the new man" (Eph. 4:24; Col. 3:10). There is no inconsistency, then, in the overall application of these two apparently contradictory principles. There is no contradiction between loving fallen human beings and recognizing our own need of renewal.

We should now be able to see the peculiar structure of Van Til's "analogical system." *All doctrines are interdependent,* in that none can be adequately understood except in the light of the others. All doctrines are "apparently contradictory," in that *none exhausts the fullness of the truth,* and their non-exhaustive character limits our ability to demonstrate formal logical consistency. Yet *all doctrines are true as far as they go,* are not "really" contradictory, and are intelligible in that even though they may be unassimilable to the forms of our logic, nevertheless provide clear guidance for God's people. This account of the nature of the Christian "system" is a theological accomplishment of immense magnitude.[130]

Epilogue

In my view, Van Til's concept of a "theological system" is his most important contribution to theology, as well as the most difficult one for most of us to understand. I trust that what I have written has clarified this concept, at least for some. I have also mentioned quite a number of Van Til's distinctive formulations of specific doctrines, each of which is important in its own right. I have discussed (in the context of our broader concern) Van Til's view of general and special revelation, his concept of the "incomprehensibility of God," and his many interesting formulations of the various kinds of "interdependence" and "paradox" found at many doctrinal loci. In these discussions, I have provided an outline of Van Til's distinctive theological positions, as well as an account of his general view of the nature and method of theology.

There is much more that could be said, however. Van Til's concept of "common grace" as "earlier" grace is highly significant and merits much close analysis.[131] His non-intellectualistic view of man's nature,[132] his view of sin as "ethical,"[133] his view of the Chalcedon Christology as a function of the Creator-creature distinction,[134] his immensely fertile account of the goal, motive, and standard of ethics:[135] all of these and others deserve close examination, analysis, proclamation. Further, a really complete account of Van Til's theology could not ignore his critiques of non-Reformed thought—critiques both interesting in themselves and useful in

---

130. See if the above account does justice to the difficult passage in *The Defense of the Faith,* 231f., where Van Til argues that temporal creation is "implied in" but not a "logical derivative from" the doctrine of God. I think myself that Van Til's concept of "implication" here is a *sort* of "logical derivation"; yet it is different enough from other types of derivation, perhaps, to merit a different name in Van Til's estimation.

131. Van Til, *Common Grace and the Gospel.*

132. Van Til, *An Introduction to Systematic Theology,* 32.

133. *Ibid.,* 24f., 253ff., elsewhere.

134. Van Til, *The Defense of the Faith,* 32ff.

135. Van Til, *Christian-Theistic Ethics.*

helping us better to formulate the doctrines in question. Van Til's critique of Barth's universalism, for instance, is instructive not only in warning us against Barth, but also in showing us the ways in which alien philosophical motifs may lead to compromise in the doctrine of definite atonement. Hopefully, other studies will be produced dealing with these matters in detail. The present study, having already exceeded the editor's length requirement, is nearly at an end. I do feel, however, that this paper demonstrates something of the immense significance of Van Til's work for the theologian, and something of the difficulty involved in understanding and appropriating it. If I am right, then I have furnished herein the best and only justification for further research into this extremely important thinker. Surely one day there will have to be a *Cornelius Van Til als Dogmaticus!*